Red Bull

LIFE AT THE
EDGE

FORMULA ONE

STEPHEN RICHARD

Ransom

FORMULA ONE CAR

Back wings.
Help press the car
down onto the track.

Air intake.
Helps cool
the engine.

Tyres.
They have no tread on them.
The tyres last just half a race.

Scuderia Toro Rosso STR 4 Data

Engine:	Ferrari V8 Type 056
Gears:	7 forward, 1 reverse
Top speed:	350 km/hour (219 mph)
Acceleration:	0 - 100 km/hour in 2.5 seconds.

Cockpit.
Made to fit
the driver.

Front wings.
Help press the car
down onto the track.

Scuderia Toro Rosso is a Formula One racing team. The team is based in Italy.

This is Sebastien Buemi ...

... and this is Jaime Alguersuari.

They are young drivers. They drive for Scuderia Toro Rosso.

Remember their names. One day they will win the World Championship.

I am a Formula One driver, too. I also drive for Scuderia Toro Rosso.

Today there is a Formula One Grand Prix race.

This is my car.

Before the race we test the car. We get it right for the track.

We do this for two days. It is hard work.

We use lots of computers to see how to go faster.

Do I brake too soon? Am I in the best gear? The computers can tell me.

We do test laps, too. The faster you go, the higher up the starting grid you are.

Now it is the day of the race.

I was the fastest car in the test laps.

So I am at the front on the grid.

This is called pole position.

OK. Now we're ready. It's the race. For real.

Five red lights go on, one by one. Then they all go off.

That's the start of the race.

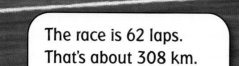

The race is 62 laps. That's about 308 km.

The first car to cross the finish line is the winner.

And right now, I'm in front.

The car is very fast.

It can go from 0 to 100 kilometres per hour in 2.5 seconds.

It is also very fast in the corners.

I must not make a mistake.

The wings on the car make down force.

This presses the car onto the track when it goes fast.

GIVES YOU WINGS

Some guys in the pits say that the car can drive upside down on the ceiling – without falling off!

That's how strong the down force is.

But I've never tried it!

The car is very light. It weighs just 605 kg – including the driver.

RedBull

Formula One cars use over 200 litres of fuel in one race.

Fuel is very heavy, so the car only carries as much as it needs.

The tyres have no treads. We call them 'slicks'.

The tyres only last for half of a race.

We must use two kinds of tyres in the race: a soft kind and a hard kind.

The soft kind has a green stripe on the tyre.

Driving these cars sounds like fun, but it is very hard work.

When I turn corners at speed, the G force makes it difficult to breathe.

The cars can pull 5G in some corners. That hurts.

So I need very strong neck muscles.

But I must focus. One mistake and I can lose my place – or crash.

I must focus like this for the whole race. I cannot relax or think of anything else!

I sit in the cockpit. It is a very tight fit.

I must take the steering wheel off to get in and out.

The steering wheel can do lots of things.

It can change gears. It can change the fuel mix and call the pits on the radio.

x10

It also has a screen to tell me speed, gear, lap times, RPM.

The steering wheel costs a lot of money.

During the race we have to make pit stops.

To change tyres and to get more fuel.

A voice on the radio tells me to go into the pits on the next lap.

I drive into the pit lane.

The pit guys show me where to stop.

A pit stop happens very quickly.

Every second in the pits is a second lost in the race.

I keep my foot on the brakes.

I keep the engine running, too.

Two guys lift the car up with jacks.

There are three guys to change each tyre.

It takes just 3 seconds to change all four tyres.

The car needs fuel, too.

Two guys put fuel in the car. They put in just enough to finish the race – or to get to the next pit stop.

When the wheels are on and the fuel is in, everything is done.

Off I go.

Back into the race. I am still in front.

Ten laps to go.

The end of the race.

And I have won the Grand Prix!

That feels as good as anything I can think of!

Everybody cheers over the radio.

On TV, when we win, I get the credit.

When we lose, I get the blame.

But in fact it is a team effort. I have to be the best. But the car must be the best too.

JARGON BUSTER

brake pressure
brakes
cockpit
computer
down force
Formula One
fuel
fuel mix
G force
gear
Grand Prix
Grands Prix
grid

kph (kilometres per
    hour)
lap
litre
pit lane
pit stop
pole position
RPM (revolutions per
    minute)
'slicks'
steering wheel
tyre